GENE EDITING

Meg Marquardt
and Blaine Wiseman

AV2

www.av2books.com

AV2

Step 1
Go to **www.av2books.com**

Step 2
Enter this unique code

JQTPSJP9H

Step 3
Explore your interactive eBook!

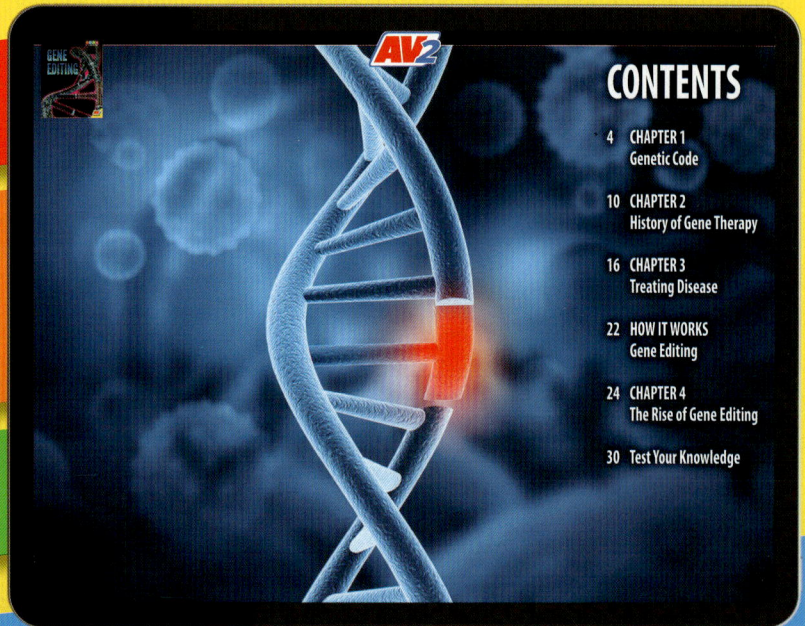

AV2

CONTENTS

AV2 is optimized for use on any device

Your interactive eBook comes with...

Contents
Browse a live contents page to easily navigate through resources

Audio
Listen to sections of the book read aloud

Videos
Watch informative video clips

Weblinks
Gain additional information for research

Try This!
Complete activities and hands-on experiments

Key Words
Study vocabulary, and complete a matching word activity

Quizzes
Test your knowledge

Slideshows
View images and captions

This title is part of our AV2 digital subscription

1-Year K–5 Subscription
ISBN 978-1-7911-3320-7

Access hundreds of AV2 titles with our digital subscription.
Sign up for a FREE trial at **www.av2books.com/trial**

GENE EDITING

Contents

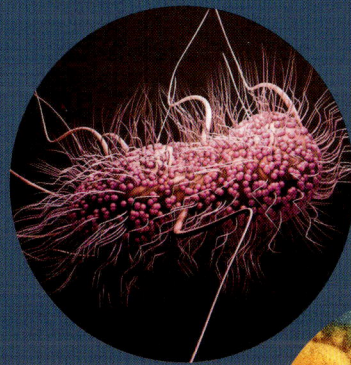

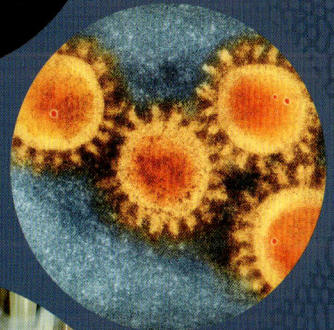

The **first** gene therapy trial took **two years** and **11 treatments** to complete.

There are about **20,000 genes** in the human body.

Scientists have found **3,230 genes** that every human needs in order to live.

Genetic Code

Scientists made history in 1990. They performed the first trial of human gene therapy. Their patient was a four-year-old girl. She had a deadly disease. The disease stopped her body from fighting illnesses. To treat the girl, the scientists had to address the root cause of the disease. They had to fix her genes.

Genes are sections of **DNA**. They are in every **cell** in the human body. DNA is like the body's instruction manual. Each gene is a different instruction. Genes tell the body to make proteins. Proteins are the body's building blocks. They are necessary for the body to function. Proteins also determine hair color, eye shape, and many other traits.

Sometimes, there are problems with a gene. A gene's instructions might be incorrect. In that case, the body might create the wrong protein or a protein that does not work. A gene can also be completely missing. If that happens, the body cannot make the protein at all. These errors can result in **genetic** disease.

STEM and the Human Body

The four-year-old girl had a genetic disease. She was missing an important gene for the **immune system**. To help her, doctors had to give her the missing gene. This process is known as gene therapy.

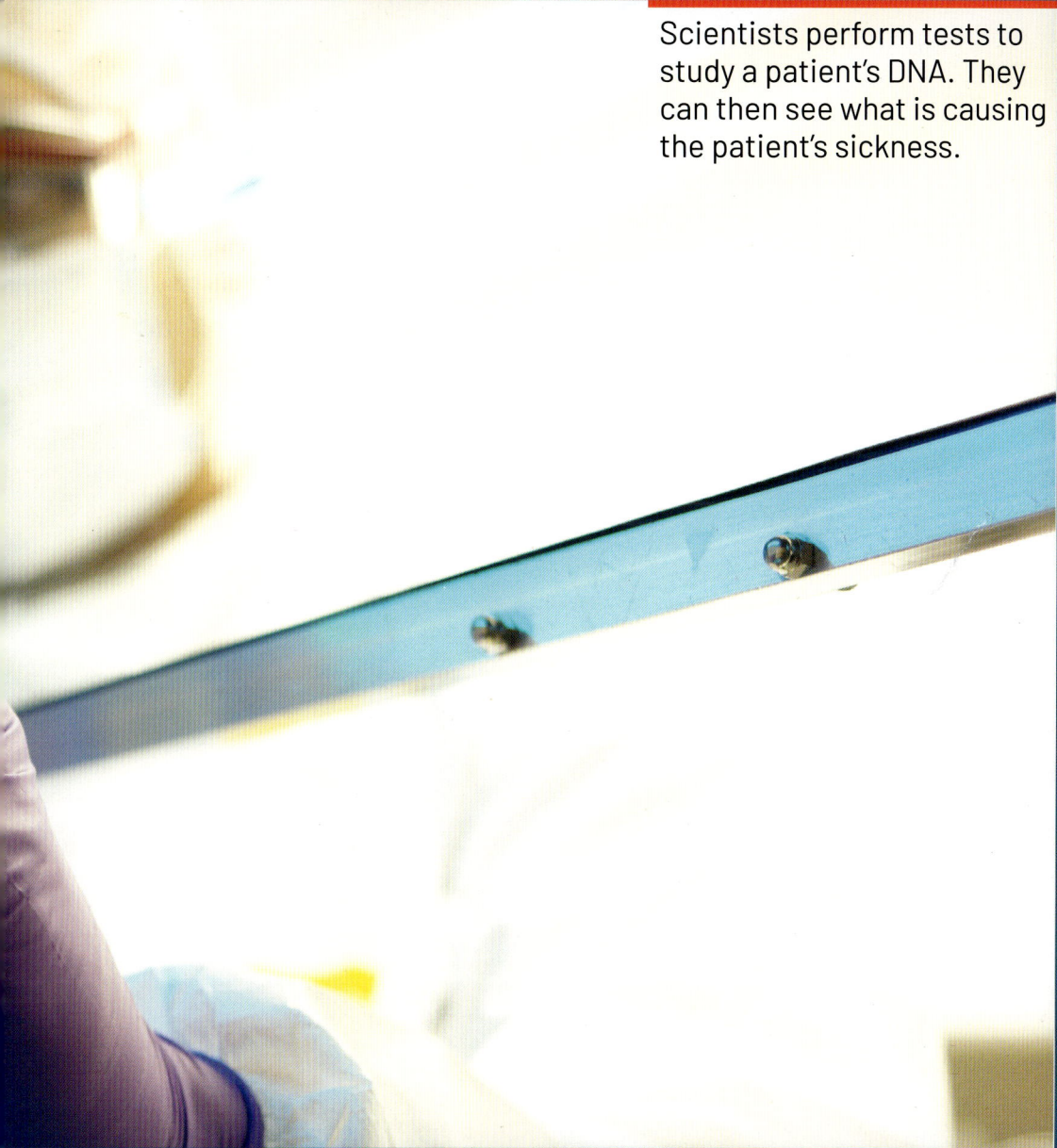

Scientists perform tests to study a patient's DNA. They can then see what is causing the patient's sickness.

First, the doctors removed some of the girl's white blood cells. These cells are an important part of the immune system. Next, the doctors inserted the correct gene into the cells. Then, they put the cells back into the girl's body.

The therapy worked. The girl's cells began creating the right protein. Her immune system began working. Her body could fight some illnesses.

However, the therapy was not a cure. The girl had to repeat the therapy every few months. Even so, she was able to live a normal life.

Gene therapies help treat genetic diseases. One type of gene therapy is called gene editing. It is a way to change DNA. It allows doctors to add or remove genes to stop problems.

Gene editing is a new technology. It is still in the early stages of research. However, it might one day help doctors treat or even cure many genetic diseases.

Scientists research gene therapy as a treatment for many diseases.

CHAPTER 2

History of Gene Therapy

Genetic research began with the study of pea plants. In the mid-1800s, Gregor Mendel saw that some peas had wrinkly skin while other peas were smooth. He found that pea plants passed this trait on to the next generation of pea plants. Similarly, children can **inherit** traits from their parents.

By the 1950s, scientists had discovered DNA. They thought that genes might be made of DNA. Genes can be passed from parent to child. They can also be passed from cell to cell.

By studying bacteria,
scientists discovered
that genes could
move between cells.

STEM and the Human Body

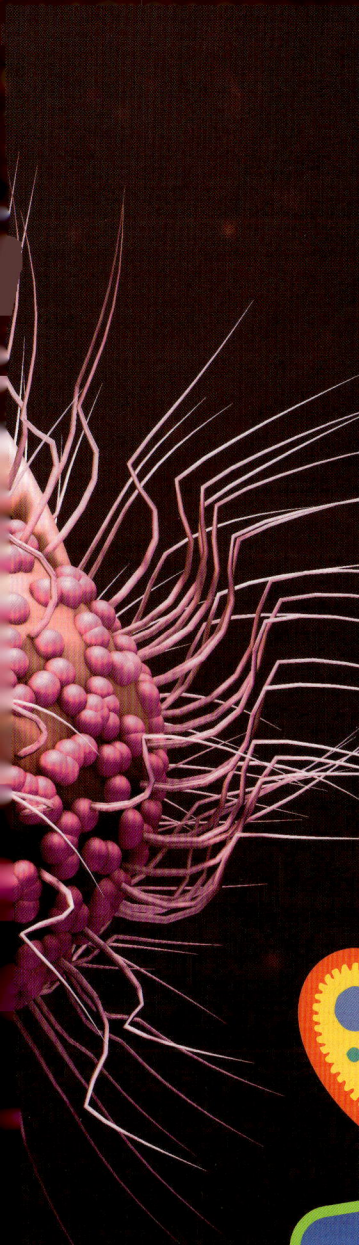

Scientists studied two groups of **bacteria**. One group reacted to drugs. The other group was **resistant**. Scientists put the two groups in the same dish. Over time, all of the bacteria became drug resistant. The bacteria had shared genes.

Scientists wondered if this discovery could be useful for humans. In the 1960s, researchers began experimenting with viruses. Viruses are good at breaking through a cell's walls. They can make people sick. However, scientists can remove the parts of viruses that cause sickness. They can use viruses as tools.

BODY CELLS VS. GERM CELLS

The human body has two main types of cells. Body cells include skin and muscle cells. When changes are made to the genes in a body cell, only the patient is affected. The changes are not passed on to the patient's children.

Germ cells are the cells that make a baby. Changes made to the genes of germ cells will affect the patient's future children. The changes will be passed down from parent to child in the **germline**.

Many viruses cause infection, but they can also be made into useful tools for gene therapy.

Scientists had an idea. They could use viruses to carry genes. Imagine a patient who is missing an important gene. Scientists could put that gene into a virus. Then, they could inject the virus into the patient. The virus would go into cells. It would deliver the missing gene. The cells would pass that gene along to even more cells. With this gene, the patient's body could start making the right protein. The body could recover from diseases.

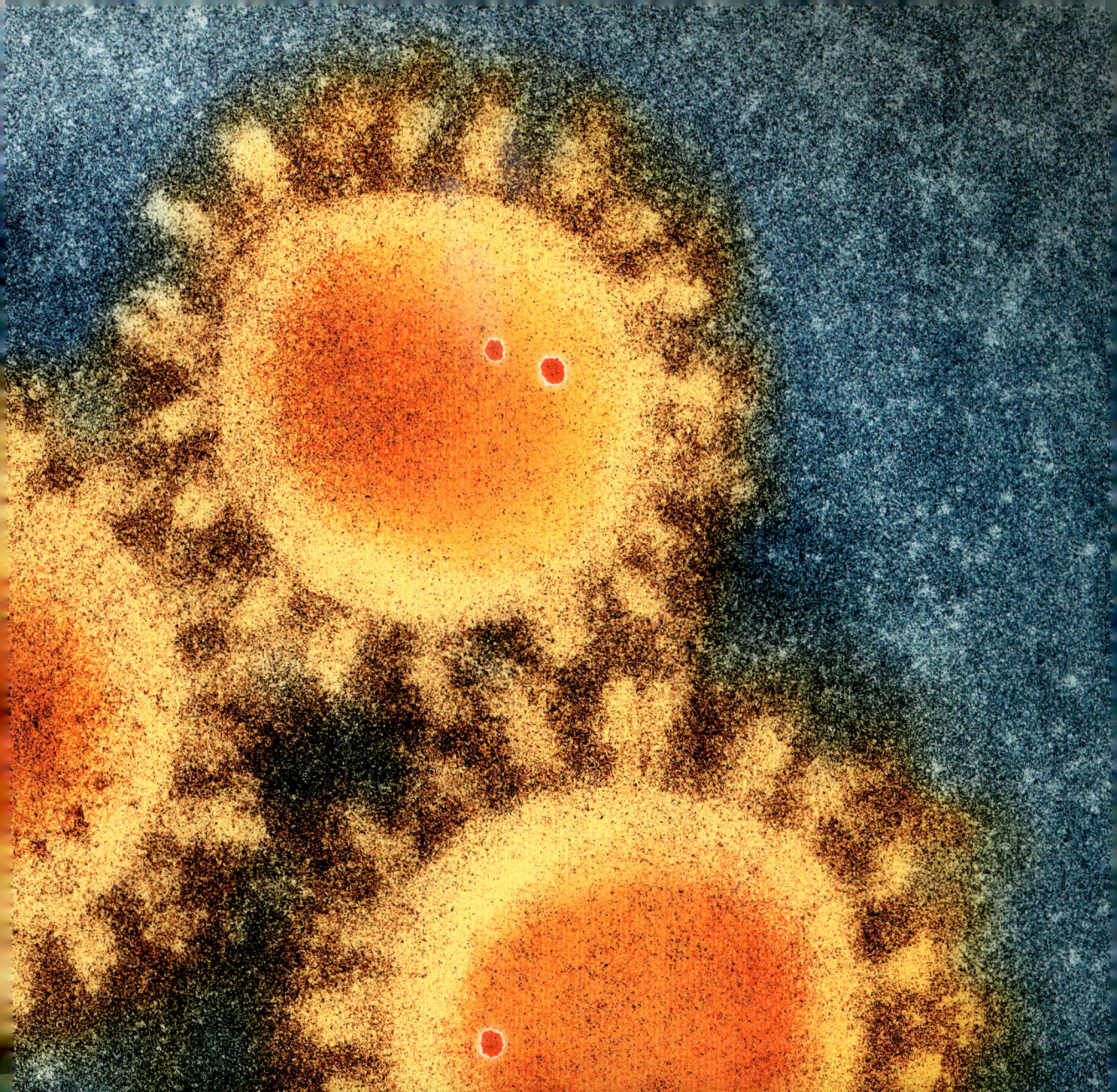

In 1990, scientists put this idea into practice. They did the first human gene therapy trial. Since then, scientists have treated other diseases with gene therapy. They continue to study ways to improve their techniques.

CHAPTER 3

Doctors hope to use gene therapy on the **p53 gene** to treat several types of cancer.

In **2018**, a pair of twin girls became the first people born with edited genes.

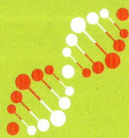

Gene therapy treatments can cost a patient more than **$1 million**.

STEM and the Human Body

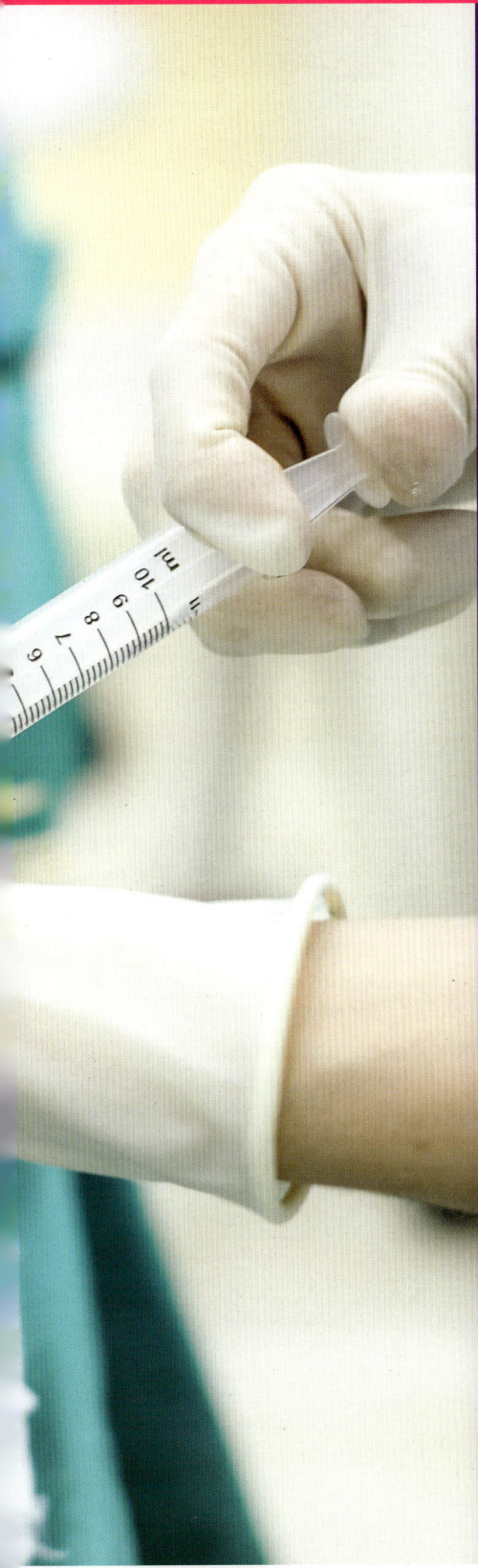

Treating Disease

Scientists have used gene therapy to treat many conditions. For example, they have used it to restore sight. They have reversed the effects of skin disease. Scientists have also treated a disease called sickle cell anemia.

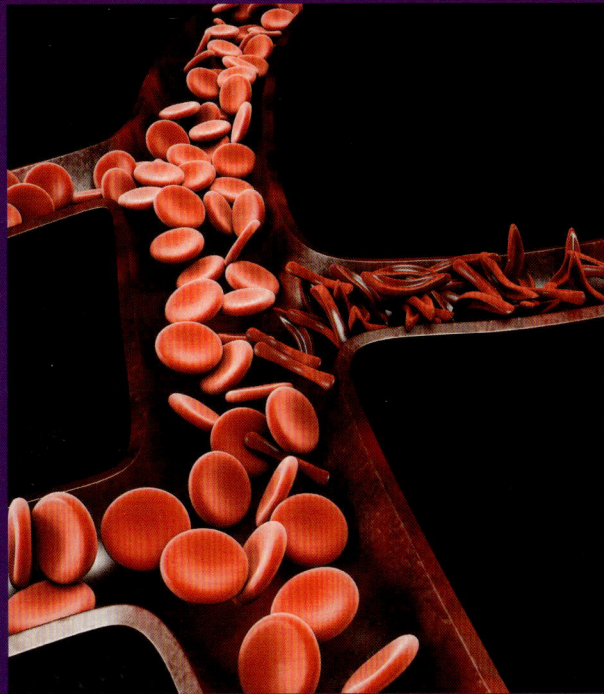

Sickle cell anemia is an inherited blood disorder. It changes healthy red blood cells into a crescent, or sickle, shape.

In sickle cell anemia, red blood cells have the wrong shape. They are thin and curved. These wrongly shaped cells are called sickle cells. Sickle cells cannot move through blood vessels easily. They get stuck. When that happens, they block oxygen from moving around the body. It takes only one small genetic change to cause this disease.

In 2017, scientists took cells from a young boy with sickle cell anemia. They gave those cells the correct red blood cell gene. Then, they put the cells back into the boy's body. After treatment, the boy's body was better at making normal cells. He still had some sickle cells, but he had more normal blood cells. The boy is now healthy because of the gene therapy.

One challenge of gene therapy is making sure the genes get to the right parts of cells. Scientists try to control where the new genes go, but they sometimes miss their target. Part of the challenge is working on such a small scale. DNA is made up of molecules. Molecules are very small.

Healthy red blood cells are round and flexible. They travel easily through blood vessels and carry oxygen to every part of the body.

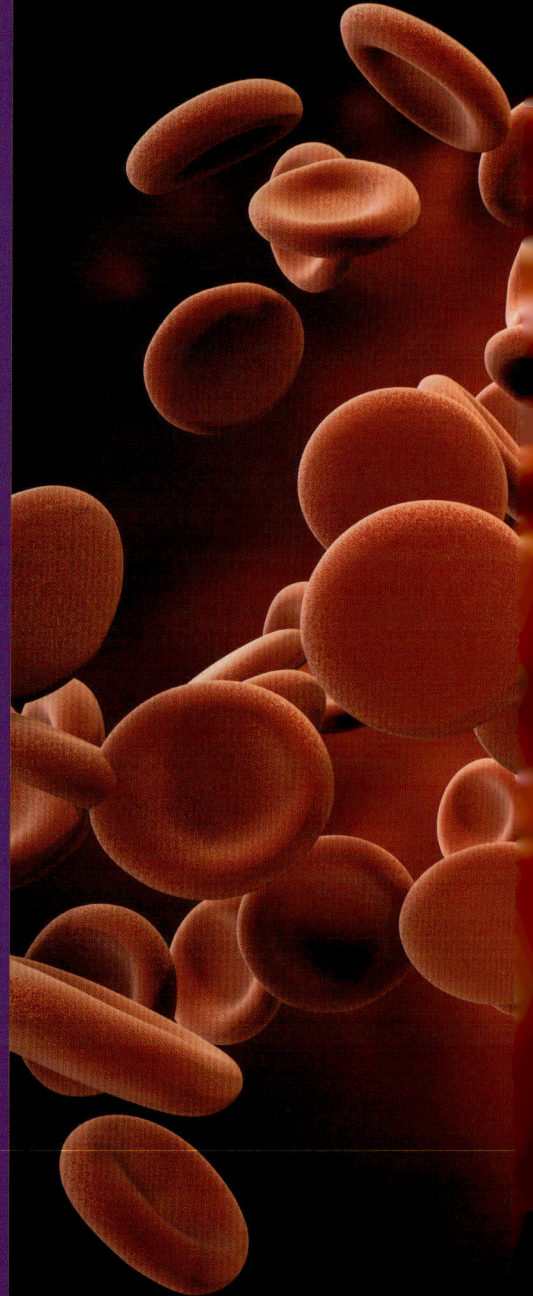

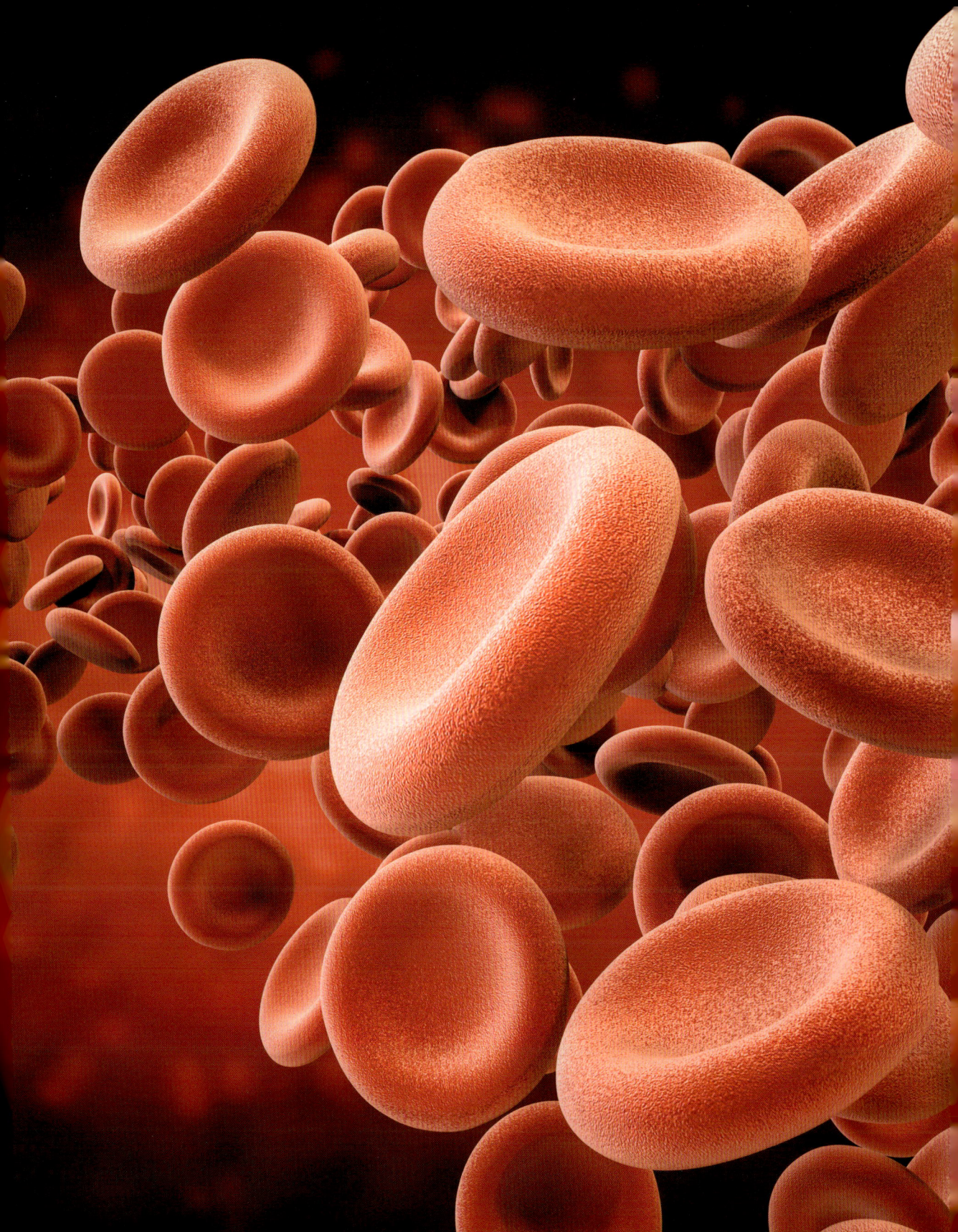

Scientists cannot see molecules without the help of specialized equipment.

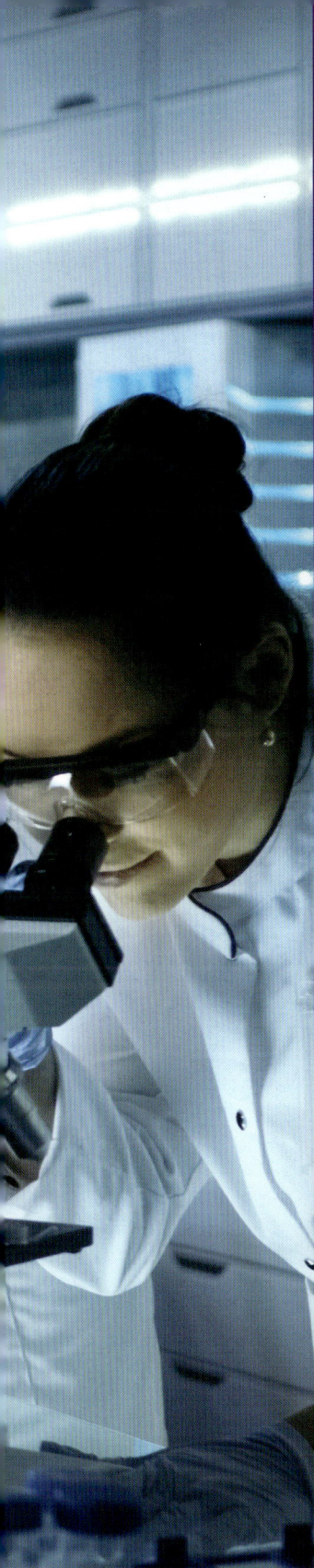

The newest form of gene therapy is gene editing. It puts these tiny molecules to work. In gene editing, scientists use molecules as guides to specific spots in the DNA. Scientists can add a new gene. They can make changes to genes already in the DNA. They can even delete bad genes. The molecule guides give scientists more control.

Understanding Genes

Genes are very complex. Scientists used to think that one gene created one protein. Now scientists know that many genes have more than one job.

Genes also affect one another. Scientists must study genes carefully to understand their effects. Editing a gene could solve one problem but cause other problems in the future.

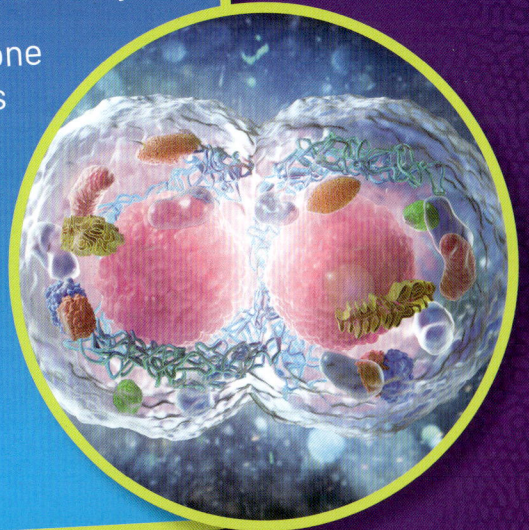

Gene Editing

Scientists use two main tools in gene editing. The first tool is a small molecule called RNA. The RNA molecule acts as a guide. Specific pieces of RNA can seek out specific genes. Scientists insert the RNA molecule into a cell. The RNA sticks to the gene that needs to be cut. It makes gene editing a precise process.

The second tool is an enzyme. Enzymes are molecules that can make changes in a cell. In this case, the enzyme cuts genes.

The RNA molecule directs the enzyme to the correct gene. The enzyme makes a cut. Different things can happen next. Sometimes, the cut ends stick together to fix the DNA. Other times, new genes can be added to the DNA.

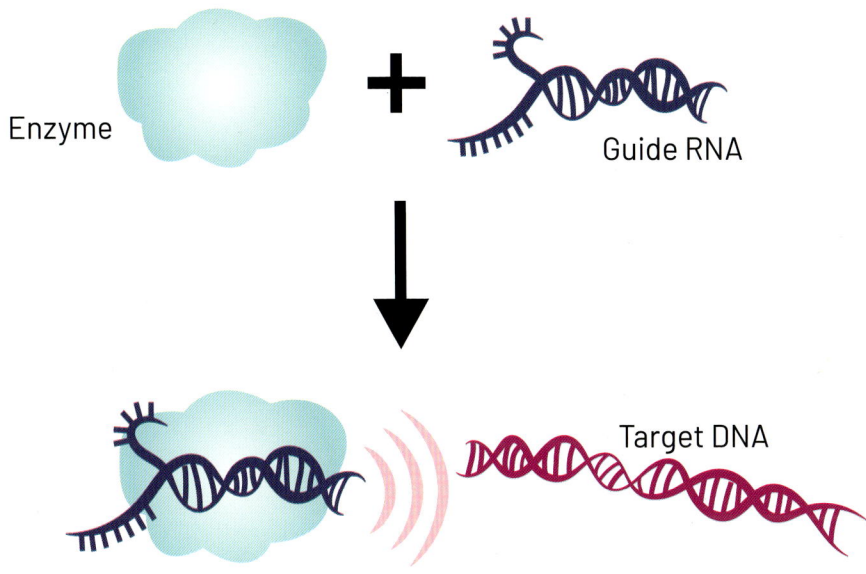

Enzyme + Guide RNA

Together, the enzyme and the guide RNA find the target DNA.

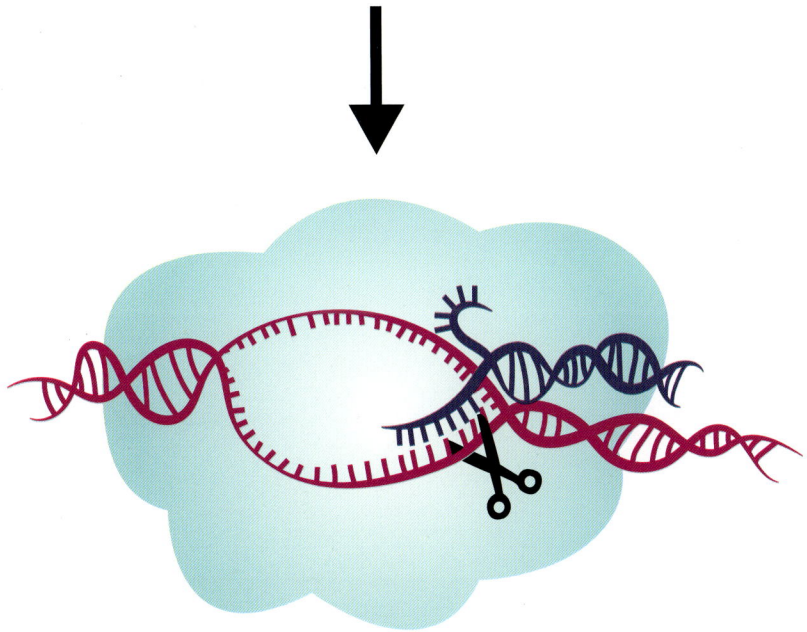

Target DNA

The guide RNA lines up with the target DNA.
The enzyme cuts the DNA.

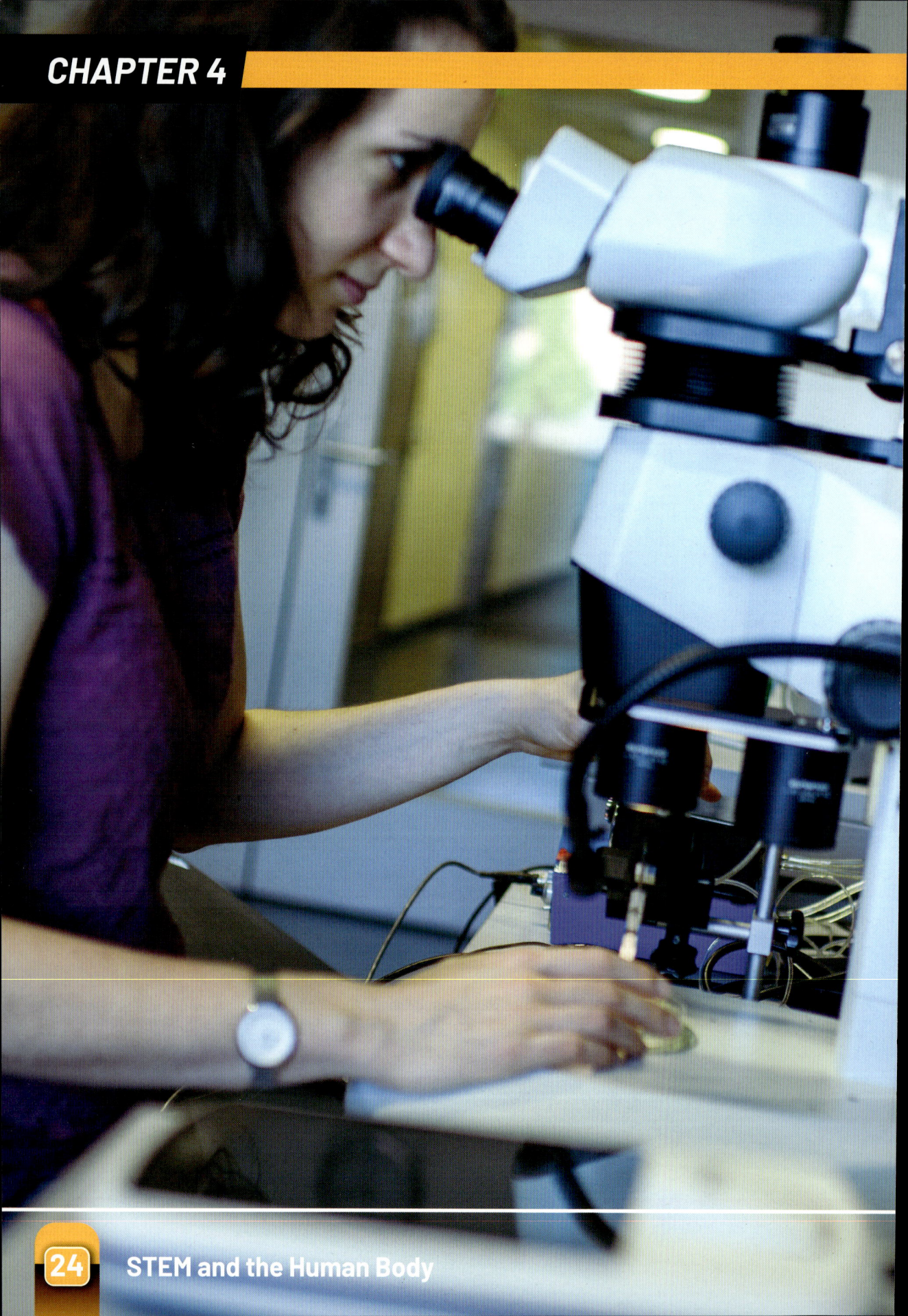

CHAPTER 4

The Rise of Gene Editing

Gene editing is a new technology. It has not been done in human patients. However, it has been done in human cells in a test tube. Scientists are also testing the process on animals.

Scientists use a new tool known as CRISPR. This tool is actually a section of DNA. It occurs naturally in bacteria. CRISPR DNA creates a protein that works to defend the bacteria. Like scissors, the protein can cut up the DNA of other organisms.

Scientists must carefully insert the CRISPR tool into cells.

Scientists saw how well CRISPR could cut up genes. They decided to use that power in gene editing. Scientists have used CRISPR to cut out specific genes. They have also used it to add new genes into a cell's DNA.

Many people hope CRISPR will help fight cancer. Cancer is often caused by a **mutation** in a gene. Sometimes, the mutated gene tells a person's immune system to not attack cancer cells. With CRISPR, scientists can cut out that gene. That way, the person's body will become better at fighting cancer.

Some scientists are thinking about doing germline editing. Germ cells are passed from parent to child. Editing these cells could stop a genetic disease. It would prevent a future child from inheriting the disease from the parents.

Most scientists are very concerned about changing germ cells. The changes would be passed down forever. An error in the gene-editing process could cause major problems to future generations.

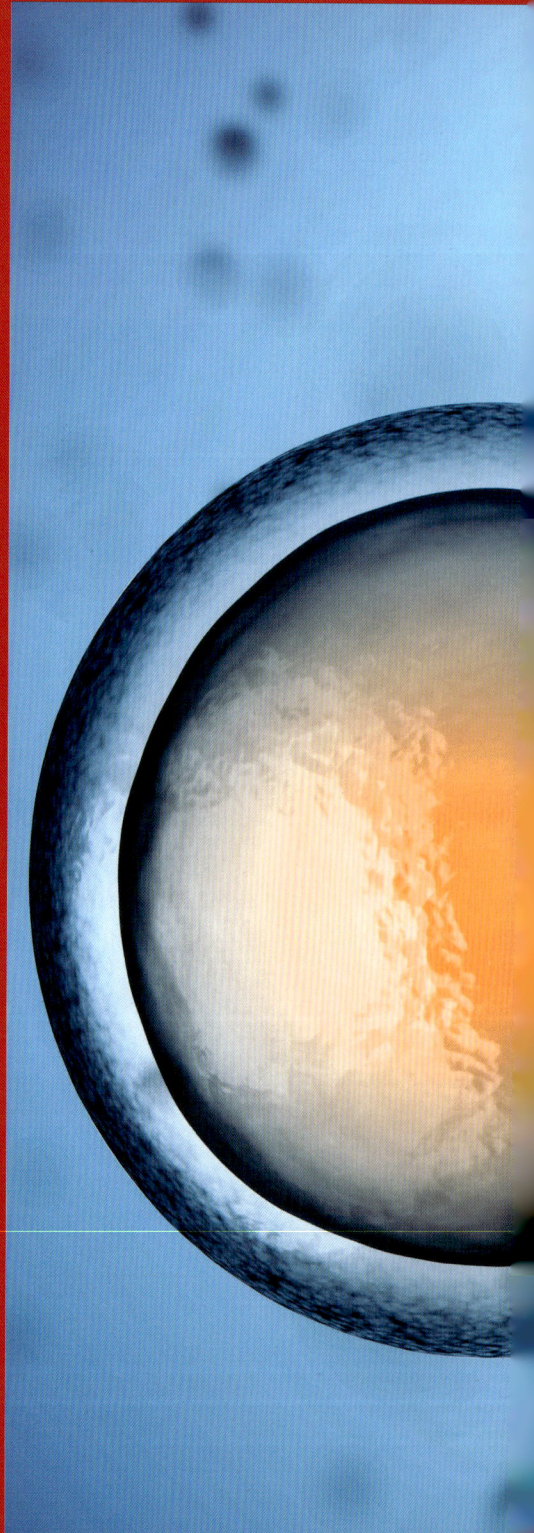

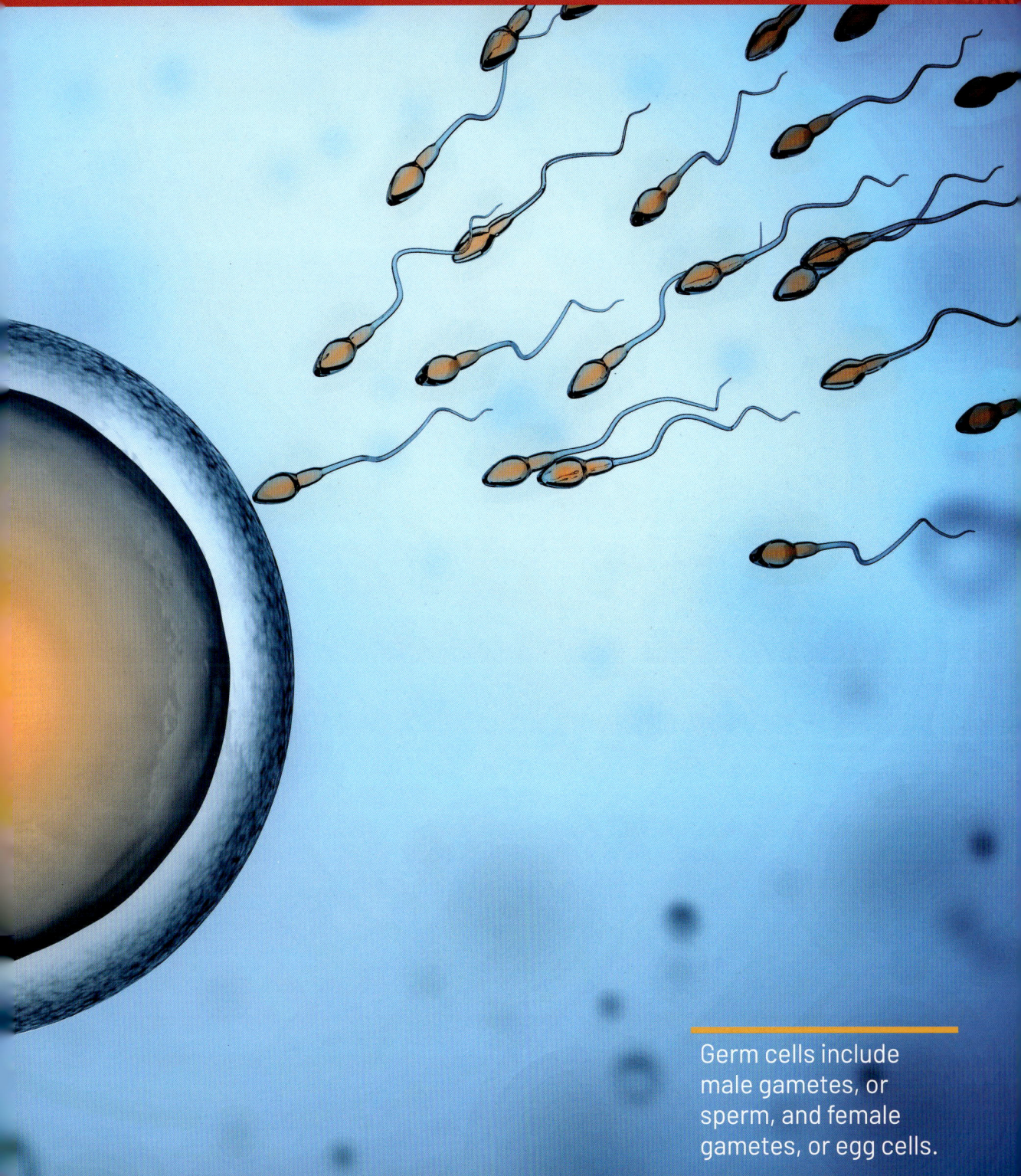

Germ cells include male gametes, or sperm, and female gametes, or egg cells.

Gene therapy could be used to treat diseases such as diabetes, cancer, and heart disease.

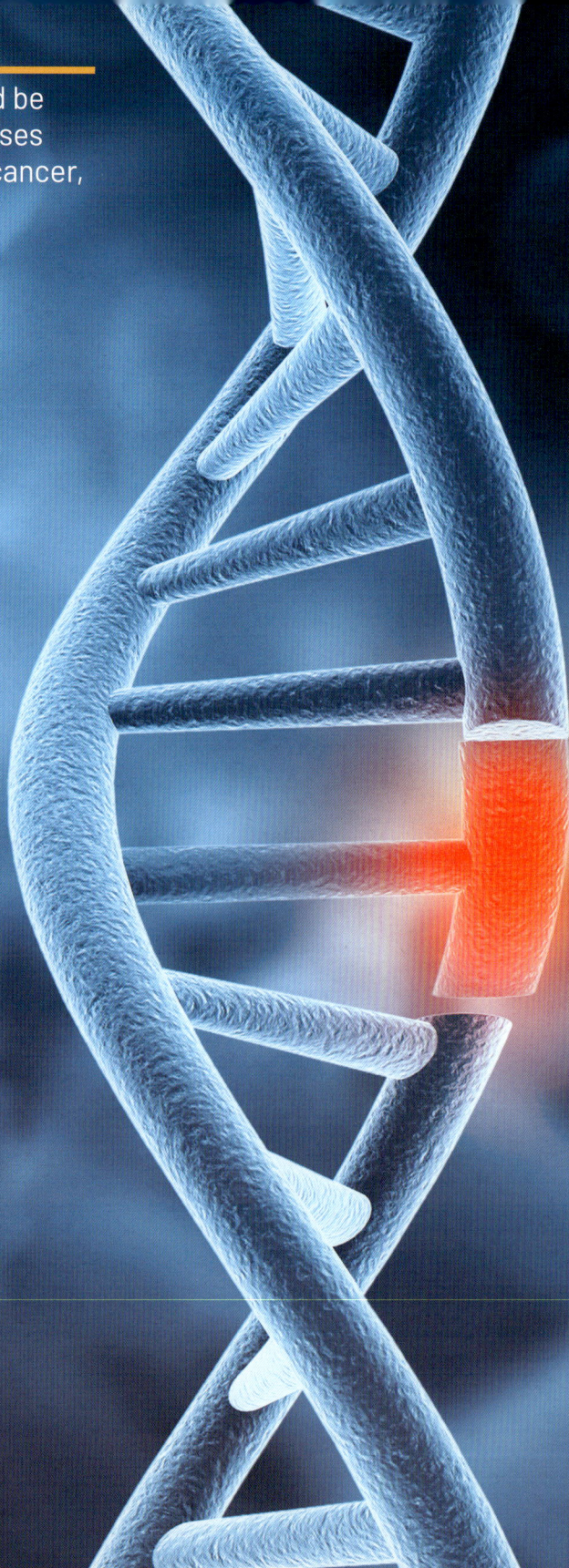

STEM and the Human Body

Gene editing faces many challenges, but it also has a great deal of promise. It might one day cure diseases. It may help scientists test better treatments. There is still much research to be done. In the meantime, other gene therapies can help treat diseases.

GERMLINE EDITING CONTROVERSY

A Chinese scientist edited the genes of human embryos. Embryos are organisms in an early stage of development.

The embryos grew into babies. They were born in November 2018. Their father has a disease. The scientist edited the embryos' genes to make them resist this disease. The scientist did this work in secret.

Many scientists around the world are concerned. Government agencies have not yet approved germline editing in humans.

Test Your Knowledge

1

What are the body's building blocks called?

A: Proteins

2

What do we call the process of giving someone a gene they are missing?

A: Gene therapy

3

What are genes and where are they found?

A: Sections of DNA; in every cell of the body

4

Who began studying gene therapy with pea plants?

A: Gregor Mendel

5

What are the two types of cells in the human body?

A: Body cells and germ cells

6

In what year did scientists use human gene therapy for the first time?

A: 1990

7

What type of gene therapy can be used to delete bad genes?

A: Gene editing

8

What two main tools do scientists use in gene editing?

A: RNA and enzymes

9

What genetic disease makes the body produce thin, curved blood cells?

A: Sickle cell anemia

10

What new gene editing tool could be used to treat cancer in the future?

A: CRISPR

Key Words

bacteria: microscopic, single-celled living things that can be useful or harmful

cell: the smallest unit of a living organism that can function and perform tasks

DNA: the genetic material in the cells of living organisms

genetic: relating to traits and molecules inherited from parents

germline: the germ cells and the changes to germ cells that are inherited through multiple generations

immune system: the body system that uses specialized cells to fight infections

inherit: to receive something from one's parents

mutation: an unexpected change in a gene

resistant: able to stop something from working

Index

Get the best of both worlds.

AV2 bridges the gap between print and digital.

The expandable resources toolbar enables quick access to content including **videos**, **audio**, **activities**, **weblinks**, **slideshows**, **quizzes**, and **key words**.

Animated videos make static images come alive.

Resource icons on each page help readers to further **explore key concepts**.

Published by AV2
276 5th Avenue, Suite 704 #917
New York, NY 10001
Website: www.av2books.com

Library of Congress Control Number: 2020937073

ISBN 978-1-7911-2416-8 (hardcover)
ISBN 978-1-7911-2417-5 (softcover)
ISBN 978-1-7911-2418-2 (multi-user eBook)
ISBN 978-1-7911-2419-9 (single-user eBook)

Printed in Guangzhou, China
1 2 3 4 5 6 7 8 9 0 25 24 23 22 21

022021
101320

Art Director: Terry Paulhus Project Coordinator: Priyanka Das

Every reasonable effort has been made to trace ownership and to obtain permission to reprint copyright material. The publisher would be pleased to have any errors or omissions brought to its attention so that they may be corrected in subsequent printings.

The publisher acknowledges Alamy, Getty Images, iStock, and Shutterstock as its primary image suppliers for this title.

First published by Focus Readers in 2020.